de Kooning: Recent Paintings

THOMAS B. HESS

de Kooning: Recent Paintings

 Walker and Company, New York

Frontispiece: *Pastorale*. 1963. Oil on canvas, 70 × 80 in. Private collection

Library of Congress Catalog Card Number 67–30380
Published simultaneously in Canada by The Ryerson Press, Toronto
Printed in the United States of America
Photographs of de Kooning by Dan Budnik
Designed by Bert Clarke

PUBLISHED BY WALKER AND COMPANY
A DIVISION OF WALKER PUBLISHING COMPANY, INC.,
IN ASSOCIATION WITH
M. KNOEDLER & CO. INC., NEW YORK

Acknowledgements

The Publishers and M. Knoedler and Company wish to express their gratitude to Mr. Joseph H. Hirshhorn, Mr. Edgar Kaufmann, jr., and Mr. John G. Powers who so generously made special contributions to the preparation of this volume and lent their paintings to the de Kooning exhibition held at M. Knoedler and Company from November 14 through December 2, 1967.

Man likes to make roads and to create, that is a fact beyond dispute. But why has he such a passionate love for destruction and chaos also? Tell me that! But on that point I want to say a couple of words myself. May it not be that he loves chaos and destruction (there can be no disputing that he does sometimes love it) because he is instinctively afraid of attaining his object and completing the edifice he is constructing? Who knows, perhaps he only loves that edifice from a distance, and is by no means in love with it at close quarters; perhaps he only loves building it and does not want to live in it, but will leave it, when completed, for the use of domestic animals—such as ants, sheep and so on. Now ants have quite different tastes. They have a marvelous edifice in a pattern which endures forever—the ant-heap.

DOSTOEVSKI, *Notes from the Underground*

Content . . . is a glimpse. . . . I guess you could call me a slipping glimpser . . .

I was reading Kierkegaard (for whom I have a great admiration) and came across the phrase, "purity is to will one thing." It made me sick.

WILLEM DE KOONING

In the spring of 1963, Willem de Kooning moved out of the big gleaming loft he had fixed up on Broadway, to live the year-round on Long Island.

Since 1951 he had spent most of his summers in East Hampton. In 1962 he bought a cottage from his brother-in-law and a piece of land nearby on which he began to build an ideal studio. But New York was still his base of operations—as it had been since 1927, one year after his arrival from Holland.

He had been a visitor to the country from time to time. Henceforth he would be a visitor to the city, and with decreasing frequency.

Before packing up, he finished the last of a series of large (70 by 80 inches) abstract paintings with a landscape feel to them; appropriately enough, he titled it *Pastorale*.

The pastoral, from Theocritus to Frost or Bly, is an urban, intellectual mode: a recollection of the country with the horseflies, mud, and dung washed out of memory. The sea is always a glittering blue-green; sunlight perpetually dances off the ever green leaves and the warm gold sand. It is never too hot or too cold. When violence makes an appearance, it comes as a poetic, natural force: the Wave pounds on the Shore, the Wind pushes through the Tree. Generalization, synecdoche, a bit of myth; dulcet.

And a pastoral is envisioned from the city, in de Kooning's case from New York, the ultimate twentieth-century mess and marvel. Remembrance of the woods or the beach is summoned up in a room looking out on Broadway's filthy sidewalks where old newspapers caked with soot fly up against the urine-stiffened pants of bums trying to dodge the trucks banging downtown with their loads of scrap iron and mattresses, while from three storys above the exhaust fans of light industry pump the air full of chemicals which stain it that infernal yellow first noticed by Baudelaire as a characteristic of the modern metropolis.

The Loft

De Kooning was one of the New York artists who "invented" loft life in the late 1920s and early 1930s. In order to solve the problem of getting a big studio he could afford, the artist rented the cheap space that had been used by small manufacturers to produce such items as taffy or celluloid dolls' heads. The next step was to clear out everything, pull down the old partitions, opening up the place, and then paint the walls white, achieving a long rectangle of light: a room as serene as the nave of a Cistercian chapel. Because it was against the law for artists to sleep in their lofts (they were and still are zoned for commercial use only, although a "gentleman's agreement" with the city now gives artists a tentative security), a bed that folded quickly into a wall became an essential part of de Kooning's shipshape furnishings, along with a wide, circular natural wood table, a few chairs, a kitchenette as neat as a sea cook's galley. The rest of the area was work space: an easel-wall (upon which the canvas was stapled; de Kooning prefers to work on a resistant surface), a heavy glass tabletop for a palette on which colors could be stored and mixed, shelving for brushes, canvas, paper, portfolios of drawings, a bulletin board on which drawings, illustrations from art books and magazines, postcards, and telephone numbers could be pinned for handy reference, and hanging someplace, a heavy-breasted calendar nude, her smile as sweet as candy, presided as the genius of the place.

The loft and its clear light had an influence on the developing styles of modern American painting. The studio itself tended to encourage an opening up of shapes, simplification and clarification of color, as well as experiments with large-scale formats. I do not think it is a coincidence that artists in, for example, Rome or San Francisco, who usually work in smaller, darker, cozier, more comfortable quarters, have produced smaller, more comfortable, slightly cramped paintings. The place where art is made affects its look; it is where the art appears at its most natural and thus at its best. It is also the place where the pressure of intentions behind the art can be most easily apprehended by a spectator. New York light (according to Matisse, it is most like the "clear saline light of Venice") is the fluid in which the cosmopolitan styles of postwar art developed; it is exemplified in New York School painting and experienced in the raw in the New York lofts.

In 1957 and 1958, as de Kooning began to sell his paintings more easily, he improved his studio, first indulging in the luxury of buying pounds of paint, boxfuls of brushes, reams of paper, rolls of canvas; finally he moved from Tenth Street to Broadway and remodeled the top floor of number 831 into the first (to my knowledge) of what could be called the "luxury lofts"—wood floors sanded and waxed, sparkling like crystal; chairs by Eames instead of homemade carpentry; a refrigerator capable of producing ice with real suburban efficiency. Other artists since have made similar transformations, changing the old loft studios, which had a strong air of the vows of poverty about them, into new luxury models, and, as might have been expected, a few collectors have also moved into these severely gracious accommodations.

Around 1958–62, there was a magic moment when de Kooning somehow became "a center of everything, without wanting it"; a sort of one-man national culture institute. The President of the United States gave him a medal, as did the National Institute of Arts and Letters. Photographs of him appeared: in newspapers looking happy, in the

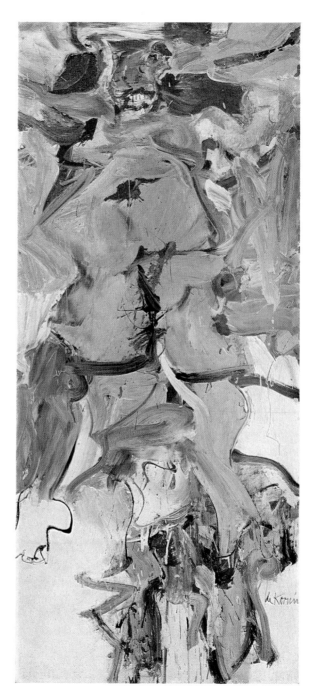

Woman Sag Harbor. 1964. Oil on wood,
80×36 in. The Joseph H. Hirshhorn
Collection

fashion magazines looking suitably bleak, and in the national news weeklies looking firmly optimistic. He was the subject of several art movies, including one handsome production in color which also featured his old friend Buckminster Fuller as well as Igor Stravinsky, and another by Hans Namuth in which some of the footage was shot through a painting with a hole cut in it, thus giving the spectator the startling impression that de Kooning was painting right over the audience's nose. He was widely quoted by admiring young artists in their work and in their catalogue forewords and by critics of every persuasion except the doctrinaire formalists, who have always attacked him. The Beat Generation poets, then at the height of their vogue, took particular trouble to include him in their pantheon.

He was introduced to Gregory Corso at a noisy party. "Are you a queer?" asked Corso. Taken aback, de Kooning said he wasn't. "Well," said the poet, "you look like one." "Well, I think you're cornball," said de Kooning and walked away, but Corso kept following him, pleading for him to come back, calling out, "Wait! I'm not a cornball; I'm very hurt; I love people." Later, at a poetry reading which de Kooning attended because his friend, the late Frank O'Hara, was on the program, Corso read a poem, "dedicated to Willem de Kooning, who's promised to give me a painting." "I'll give you a reproduction," de Kooning shouted from the audience. There was a small riot. "It was very silly, but I felt excited," said de Kooning as he described leaving the hall and his final shot at the podium, a favorite quotation from *The Horse's Mouth* (some ladies ask the hero, Gulley Jimson ["I've known lots of old nut artists like him," said de Kooning] to comment on their amateur watercolors, and Gulley, at a loss for words, finally blurts out, "They're like a fart through a keyhole!").

I cite this anecdote to indicate something of the attraction of de Kooning's growing fame to almost everybody on the make—and certainly the Beat poets, when they first made the scene, knew how to climb with the agility of chamoix.

Goodbye to New York

De Kooning got a kick out of being a focus of attention and naturally was pleased that his paintings were beginning to sell for at least a fraction of their value. In 1960, paintings by the Italian artist Afro fetched higher prices than de Koonings of the same size, despite the latter's generally acknowledged international stature; until very recently European art commanded the almost undivided attention of American collectors. But the drain that being a celebrity put on his time and energy was becoming more and more irritating. Once de Kooning offered to let his landlord raise the rent on the condition that he would *not* put in an elevator—anything to discourage the intruders who came beating at his door: plain lion-hunters, under-the-counter dealers, free-lance photographers and reporters, M.A. candidates on the prowl to pick up a good quote, equally dedicated but less easily classifiable people on the prowl to pick up a stray drawing. A good deal of the artist's time was spent just yelling through his door that he wasn't going to let the haphazard visitor in.

In addition to these exasperations, the New York art world itself had become different. Why it changed is the subject for another essay. But the *hows* are fairly evident. Primarily, the communications media—the most dynamic element in modern capitalism —began to attack the milieu. Ideas no longer emerge in a dialectical tension between antithetical forces, but simply gush into being on television, in newspapers and magazines. For a month or two, or a year or two, a new style supplies gimmicks to the fashionable designers, hostesses, politicians, and museum directors. Then it is superseded by the next hot news. And the point that the art world is a place where things are happening (and I use the participle advisedly) was not lost on the famously mobile elements of the classless American society. The new breed of collector made his appearance; he collects artists instead of art; the appearance of a painter at his dinner table becomes the content of the picture on the dining room wall. Furthermore, the art world proved to be an efficient pressure chamber from which the collector could emerge in a position for serious social climbing.

At first the communications media and new collectors concentrated on Abstract Expressionism, and in particular on de Kooning, abandoning in the process their old loyalties to Raoul Dufy, Utrillo, and Chagall for mantelpiece decoration and Diego Rivera or Bernard Buffet for heart balm. But the intellectual difficulties of the style soon put off the avant-garde audience. It did not want to be involved in anxieties, questions, subversive thinking, chaos, mystery. By 1963, attention became polarized around two styles of painting: Pop Art and the stained-color school. A typically shrewd stroke of chic was the United States representation to the Venice Biennale in 1964, which presented both together even though the assumptions of each should inevitably exclude the other.

Simultaneously, the social glue which had bound the New York art world closely together for some twenty years began to dissolve. Certainly the news media with their star-making processes affected the atmosphere. But then the artists themselves were already getting a little bored with their relentlessly enthusiastic conversations which had lasted for two decades. The idea of privacy suddenly became as important as the exercise of dialogue. As men become older, the issue narrows into the one of life and death, where private, rather than public, ideas are important.

Certainly the deaths of many key painters and sculptors left tragic gaps in the artists' community. Especially missed were the voices of Franz Kline, Hans Hofmann, and David Smith; and the daydream of what Jackson Pollock or Arshile Gorky might have done, had they survived the accidents of their deaths, was particularly poignant to witnesses of the scene.

De Kooning withdrew from New York for many reasons; I have suggested some of them, but no matter how he arrived at his decision, *Pastorale* is like a letter to a friend telling of the artist's high expectations for a life in the country.

Pastorale

In this painting, the light is still of the city and its close suburbs—the landscape that wheels by as you drive back to town, the parkways, ramps, overpasses. And some of the violence in the paint handling, particularly the thrown and spattering energy at the angles which burst out from the central horizontal action, conveys de Kooning's response to the city and its energy, style, and madness. "What an insane government," he once said, only half joking. "They tell everybody to build bomb shelters and the same day they build a bridge that's so fragile it looks like it's made out of crystal." It is the kind of painting that has given a profound meaning to the phrase "New York School," with its implications of turbulence, harshness; the rough, uncomposed, antistyle look.

De Kooning was one of the first Americans to lead the revolt, in the mid-1940s, against the cuisine refinements of School of Paris painting, in which the pigment itself —the *matière*—is lovingly patted into place, adjusted to a lush, ingratiating esthetic. He never indulged in the coarse, chauvinist, anti-French attacks so common in bars and galleries in the 1940s, which were led by Pollock and his followers, and which Pollock had received from his teacher, Thomas Benton. For de Kooning, modern art is international cosmopolitan—but with a location: New York. De Kooning's radical departure was toward a controlled Expressionism which holds the image to the surface, but reveals the drama of the destructive forces and anxieties that went into its conception. The esthetic of Paris painting was replaced by a sense of ethical pressure. A shape is finally left alone on the canvas only when it conforms as nearly as possible to the deepest sensation within the artist—to the interiorized motif.

"De Kooning keeps all the paint in front of the picture," a painter once remarked, and de Kooning comments, "I considered that a great compliment."

There are no planes or interlocking parts or harmonizations or adjustments in de Kooning's works. He strives to bring the image "there," in front of you; it has an object quality, as if a slice of reality had just been dumped into the middle of the room.

Pastorale marks the end of a series of abstractions which began around 1956 when the last of his Women opened up, becoming so interpenetrated by the background landscape elements that the figure itself turned into a landscape. *Pastorale* also signals a new beginning: the emergent shape of a standing figure can be seen if it is assumed for a moment that the left-hand side of the picture is the top (and it should be recalled that de Kooning usually paints his pictures from all sides, turning them around on his

Woman Acabonic. 1966. Oil on paper,
80×36 in.

painting wall and often not deciding which is the top until the painting is almost finished). The idea of Woman is also indicated by the key color, a sun-struck flesh paint. The body is a hill. The legs are cut by tree-trunk verticals. The curves of her breasts are echoed in the sky.

Woman in the Country

For the next two years, while preoccupied with building his studio, de Kooning worked on figure studies: many drawings, a few pastels, a series of oils on paper, and finally a group of large Women in narrow vertical formats.

De Kooning is a highly intellectual, analytical artist with a brilliantly original turn of mind. He has the courage to reject all *données* and to take up an issue at its most difficult formulation—he accepts the puritan alternative of grasping a sword by its blade. The ambiguities, mysteries, and chaos underlying all life (and all art), which can be expressed verbally only in near-clichés, such as, knowing more is knowing less, or, the greater the skill, the greater the difficulty, are as much the motives of his art as are the hard-won formal breakthroughs of his style. He has unlimited ambitions for his art; he wants to hit the jackpot, to include everything—except the idea of exclusivity. It is (as will be indicated later in this essay) the Renaissance, man-centered view: the artist dedicated to his own fullest development as an individual, even if it must lead to failure, or, as Giacometti put it, to painting a picture which you know beforehand is impossible.

A tension of contradictions informs every aspect of de Kooning's paintings; when there is apparently smooth sailing ahead, he will find ways to invoke peril.

The earlier abstract landscapes were clued to that peculiar, but typically mid-century topology which has grown up in between the city and the country—not quite the suburbs, with their overprotected dogwoods, but those borderland flats and meadows of debris which would look like Siberia if a line of skyscrapers didn't interrupt the horizon. It is a vast, almost invisible space of in-between (you read a newspaper when you pass it in a train; you look at the road or your companions when you drive through it). And indeed, de Kooning's content, and the modernity of his vision, involves a concentration on these "leftover" landscapes.

In his pictures of 1963 and 1964, he picked up a theme he had treated in 1952: the space in between the land and the ocean. The earlier works were titled *Women on a Dock*. Now he chose the beach, the Woman in a rowboat, or wading, or digging clams.

He became fascinated by the shimmering reflections which the water casts on the figure, the flesh rippling under the light bouncing off the bobbing wavelets. Short golden strokes of paint activate the surface of the paintings, giving them a blond and breezy Rubens air, which reminded the artist of one of his pet anecdotes about the master—Rubens' recipe for figure painting: first you work in charcoal from plaster casts of antique sculptures, for years and years, until you really can draw the body; then you bring in the live model, the pretty, warm nude, "and put in the dimples."

In these sketches, the dimples are reflections and reflections of reflections; the body above the water, mirrored in the water, seen through the water. It recalls Monet's heroic reconstitution of his water garden, except here the garden is a girl.

Some drawings in charcoal define a line that can shimmer. On one of the sheets, de Kooning wrote, "Plenty of trembling, but no fear." And it is true that the Kierkegaardian anxiety seemed for the first time to be draining out of his work; Harold Rosenberg was correct in describing these Women as "light girlies." I don't think a pun was intended, but it works anyhow, because the search in these pictures is for light—a new country light, as against the city light of the older pictures. And in order to find it, de Kooning's image of a woman who is as fierce as a hurricane was momentarily subsumed in some nymphs as blond and as debonair as Watteau's. But Woman was soon to be invoked again, in all her ferocity.

The Doors

In the spring of 1964, de Kooning found a local manufacturer of doors and he ordered some panels to his favorite height of eighty inches, and three feet wide, a narrower format than he had ever used before. As his sketches evolved into a new concept of Woman in country light, he began to enlarge them to an heroic scale (de Kooning's Woman is almost always depicted as seated; if she stood up, she'd be about ten feet tall).

As always with his methodology, elaborate workings and reworkings were needed to approach the image. There were drawings, drawings transferred to parts of the painting, tracings of parts of the painting made on drawings to be studied, cut apart, reversed, upended, put back into the picture, destroyed, recaptured. One of the results of this process was a series of works the artist called monotypes, and as these have been widely disseminated and are of a special technical interest, they merit separate consideration.

For years, de Kooning has been accustomed to sticking sheets of newspaper over sections of a work in progress: sometimes it was to cover up a certain area of the picture to get it out of the way while he was working on another part; sometimes it was to keep the paint from drying too fast.

In such paintings as *Attic* (1949), *Gotham News* (1955), and *Easter Monday* (1956), the ink on the newspaper offset into the paint, leaving columns of type, advertisements, headlines, illustrations of bathing beauties and gangsters, and so forth. De Kooning liked the effect and never bothered to erase these rather ghostly evidences of a technical process. For art historians interested in footnotes, they are the first introduction of Pop Art imagery into Abstract Expressionism, and their entirely random, anticompositional

17

Women Singing I.
1966. Oil on paper,
36×24 in.

Woman with a Hat. 1966. Oil on paper,
50×21 in.

disposition preceded the first Rauschenbergs by about a decade. Obviously de Kooning's big impact on such artists as Rauschenberg, Oldenburg, Rosenquist, and others was in the bluntness and power of his total image, which has a correspondence to such stars of popular culture as the big Lucky Strike bathing beauties which used to drive around town on the sides of mail trucks. If Rauschenberg picked up the newsprint-offset idea from de Kooning's paintings, it was through his own insight, as if he had found it for himself in nature—on a dirty wall or a badly laundered shirt. As Elaine de Kooning has pointed out, for an artist the works of his elders are part of his nature.

In the fall of 1964, de Kooning was again working with newspaper sheets, applied to the large panel where Woman was taking form. At first it was simply a way to slow down the drying of the paint so it would still be fresh when he next attacked it. Then he began to study the effect of pressing the paper on the paint, and sometimes before pulling it off, he would give the sheet a little nudge to the side, causing the pigment beneath to shift a fraction of an inch. In painting over some of the area, and leaving the rest smooth, he achieved a new variation on the "impossible" jumps of brushstroke which have characterized his work since the 1930s. This method is used for its own sake, certainly, and adds a sense of mystery and complication to the surface. But, more importantly, it helps to break up the traditional European ideal of parts of a picture fitted into a composed whole. Where Pollock exploded the faceted Cubist plane by throwing and dripping pigment, de Kooning struggles to dissolve the building unit of classical art into the sinews of the paint itself.

One cannot overemphasize the importance of de Kooning's revolutionary approach to the traditional European concepts of a painting as a balanced design: a poised system of analyzed elements each disposed as in a well-planned esthetic machine. For him, the painting must be a totality, "all of a piece," without parts or structured harmony. And, along with Pollock, Kline, Newman, and his other friends who together and separately founded the new styles of American painting, he made the unitary quality of the painting a critical function of the fullness and accuracy with which it expresses the artist's most inward experience. All other esthetic values are jettisoned to bring this sensation across. A difference to be noted, however, is that with such men as Pollock and Newman, exclusion of traditional techniques (perspective, foreshortening, impasto, modeling) was a part of the artist's metaphysics, while for de Kooning, the urge is to include everything, to give nothing up, even if it means working in a turmoil of contradictions. And, as has been suggested, a turmoil of contradictions is his favorite medium.

To return to the monotypes; because they preserve an offset paint image of the picture at a certain moment of its evolution, de Kooning saved many of them, keeping the sheets scattered on the floor around the painting area, or on shelves, to be consulted as a record of the changes the painting had gone through. They became a kind of secret visual diary, fragile evidences of the creative and destructive stages of the work in progress.

A number of dealers were able to persuade the artist to put the monotypes on the market, and they have been exhibited widely in New York and California, sometimes with rather misleading captions which suggest that they are paintings. As a matter of fact, there is not a touch of the paintbrush on most of them. This does not necessarily detract, of course, from their interest or quality.

The term *monotype* is perhaps misleading for these works, since it implies that de Kooning consciously set out to make a series of prints. Recently he has suggested they be called decals or countertypes.

The full-scale Women of 1964–66 face you directly. Visage, torso, and waist are arranged on a vertical axis with the legs supporting, from a twisted M-shape, the upward thrust of the image. The arrangement is a bit like a totem pole, or a ceremonial spear.

Face, breasts, and sex are pulled apart; the eyes twist away from the nose, the mouth is forced open in a gape, revealing dangerous teeth ("who shows me her teeth, shows me her bones," wrote Charles Lamb), the breasts point outward like arms or elbows. It is a gesture of ferocious display, as if the Woman must reveal everything, or perhaps we are required to witness the completeness of her equipment. Sometimes she is in a half-squatting position, like an eager Charleston dancer, sometimes she sits with her knees spread wide. The anatomy is cut apart and reassembled, and sections are visualized from different points of view. The feet, for example, are often seen as if one were lying on a couch, legs up on an arm, the extended toes spread a little apart. They look long, splayed, flattened, like the feet of a Christ nailed to the cross. It is not a Cubist multiple-view, but rather a presentation of the specific angle from which each part of the body is the most itself, and is most like de Kooning's idea—and the painting's requirements. Some of the Women wear big, lumpy hats, like cushions or loaves of bread, which block off the top of the picture. The anatomy generally fills the whole narrow format, like a closet packed to bursting. There is no background, only a brief indication of exterior space which writhes with an energy even more muscular than that of the figure itself. The edge of the picture has an arbitrary, cutoff quality which heightens the frontal pressure of the image.

De Kooning's Women of the 1950s were very much a part of the city. They usually sat in the artist's studio. Often a rectangular shape appears above one shoulder which could be a window either looking out (in which case the figure is indoors) or looking in (which would put her in front of a house), or it could be a shelf with objects upon it. The light was that particular New York glare which is half artificial, even on the balmiest days, and bleached still further by the whitewashed walls of the loft. And her "background," to use an old-fashioned word, was also drawn from the city.

Frank O'Hara once met de Kooning hurrying back to his studio on Tenth Street. "I've been out to buy some environment," said the painter, pointing to a blue box of Kleenex under his arm. Objects familiar to the studio (packages of food, an alarm clock,

coffeepots, cans of paint remover, drop cloths, drawings pinned to the easel), the view from his window to the street or to the backyard, are the clues to the properties around the New York Women.

When he moved to the country, for the first time he began to fill the abstract space of Woman with *plein air* light.

Series of drawings and oil-on-paper sketches indicate the beginning of ideas for a rural environment—trees, rocks, a low hill covered with bushes, tangled undergrowth, the beach, grass.

In the city, de Kooning evolved his metaphors of "no-environment" and "intimate anatomy" (which this writer has discussed at some length in an article in 1951, and in a monograph on the artist published in 1959). His insight to the former came with the realization that places in the city have no specific character which can be retained by an image. There is an anonymity, gigantic but without scale, to the New York scene. A photograph of a crowd in Madison Square Garden, to give a simple example, could be a crowd in Yankee Stadium, because both are so big that the lens cannot comprehend them. The scene is too wide to have the fact that overhead there is a roof, or there are stars, as a part of the picture. And, even on a smaller scale, there is a sameness and uniform newness about everything: the corner of a skyscraper could be a corner inside a stockbroker's parlor. The little Italianate villa turns out to be a huge water tower on top of a department store. The city is too big to give specific character to scale, and thus its salient quality becomes the interchangeability of its parts. What makes it New York is that it is no place. Probably this is a very European feeling about New York; an observation by men who are used to old cities where each square has its bookfuls of associations. Both Arp and Giacometti told me that what impressed them most about New York is how fast they got lost in it, because there are no European-type landmarks. Its thousands of buildings, of every shape, size, and color, suggest that each is something else. ("It's all so vulgar and prosaic that it borders on the fantastic," in the words of Dostoevski's *A Raw Youth*.) The insight fits perfectly, of course, into de Kooning's general metaphysics of ambiguity and of places in between. And it is also a sharp comment on our situation, without the usual American nostalgia for the present. But since moving to Long Island, de Kooning seems to have relinquished his no-environment idea in favor of looking for specific rural places and individual traits.

Like most Dutchmen, he is an enthusiastic bicycle rider, and the countryside around The Springs has reminded several visitors of Holland: a similar flatness with low rises and an expectation of the Atlantic beyond; similar clumped trees and evenly tilled fields. De Kooning says that this may be so—only he does not remember the Dutch landscape that well (he has not been back since he left in 1926). Certainly Long Island has the 180-degree horizons and tidy wildness of a van Ruysdael or a Hobbema.

Opposite: *Woman with a Green and Beige Background*. 1966. Oil on paper, 28×23 in.

"The land around my place," said de Kooning, "is covered with scrub oak, skinny trees that last only about fifty or sixty years; then they die, then grow up again. So the place looks pretty much now as it did centuries ago, in the Stone Age, when the Indians were here. So that's Timelessness! Scrub oaks. Isn't it strange, with all the romantic talk about the Timeless, that it's really commonplace?"

The "commonplace" landscape suggests an echo of his no-environment concept. But the latter is man-made, and it is most anonymous when it makes the largest claims. It has a different kind of wonder about it. In the country, on the other hand, each commonplace view is full of its own character. But de Kooning was yet to create a shape for these identities in his mind.

In order to put a mark on canvas, de Kooning has to pull it out of himself. He is a great inventor of forms. And of colors. He explained once how he could mix a color that was exactly like sand, or like the sea, or like grass. You could hold the color up to nature and it would disappear inside. But once he gets this *trompe-l'oeil* effect, he has to "make it abstract" so that he can use it again. The same holds for shapes. And probably one of the reasons why the first large Women of 1964 were planned on narrow panels is that he wanted the anatomy to fill the whole surface, because he had no background, or environment to fit.

In the background, of course, are the possibilities for giving a figure a monumental scale. And when this is eliminated, the figure tends to an icon, Byzantine look. De Kooning played with the idea, for a time, of assembling the panels of Women in a polyptych, like the parades of saints in Greek monastery frescoes. But to make a multiple painting, each part has to yield a bit of its identity to the ensemble. And each of de Kooning's Women is filled with such a savage egocentricity that the scheme had to be abandoned. They do look well together, in the studio, leaned against the table, flush with each other, but they sing much better alone.

Drawings, Inside Out

Critics and historians generally consider drawing to be the intellectual side of art (remembering the authority of Ingres and Degas, and how pupils in academies are "taught" to draw), and color, the emotional one (viz. the "passionate" yellows of van Gogh). Actually, as Fairfield Porter has pointed out, it usually is the other way around: artists invent highly rational systems for color, formulas and doctrines; while the drawing, at the edges of form, is where the most spontaneous activity takes place. Artists who wish to tap the subconscious usually try to reach it through the medium of the moving, linear stroke (Klee, Pollock). Only recently have such painters as Rothko and Newman liberated color from doctrine and used it as an instrument to probe within the psyche.

Untitled. 1966–67. Charcoal, 18¾×23¾ in.

Untitled. 1966–67. Charcoal, 23¾×18¾ in.

Untitled. 1966–67. Charcoal, 18¾×23¾ in.

Untitled. 1966–67. Charcoal, 23¾×18¾ in.

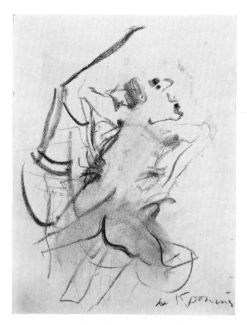

Untitled. 1966–67. Charcoal, 18¾×23¾ in.

Untitled. 1966–67. Charcoal, 14×17 in.

Untitled. 1966–67. Charcoal, 18¾×23¾ in.

Untitled. 1966–67. Charcoal, 23¾×18¾ in.

Untitled. 1966–67. Charcoal, 18¾×23¾ in.

Untitled. 1966–67. Charcoal, 18¾×23¾ in.

Untitled. 1966–67. Charcoal, 18¾×23¾ in.

Untitled. 1966–67. Charcoal, 17×14 in.

27

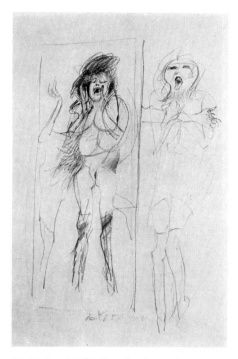

Untitled. 1966–67. Pencil, 18×12. in.

Untitled. 1966–67. Charcoal, 18×12 in.

Of course, the mind is not a mansion divided into rooms, some labeled *Emotions,* and others *Ideas.* Furthermore, intellectual processes in the visual arts proceed along the disciplines of a nonverbal logic—which can be compared to that of the mathematician who can only think when he is writing down signs on the blackboard. And, as Focillon has written, there is a brain in the hand which, while drawing, will criticize, improvise, invent, erase—think new thoughts.

For de Kooning, drawing is all of these things at once. He is a natural draftsman who draws continuously: to find new shapes, to refine a form, to be able to visualize it; he transfers drawings to the painting, or traces a section of the picture on a sheet of paper in order to study it. When he stops looking at the painting on which he is at work, he looks around his work space which is usually papered with related studies.

The drawings he has executed in the past four years on Long Island, which number in the hundreds, are among the most remarkable he, or any modern artist, has ever done. Some are pastels, a few are done in hard pencil—for years a favorite medium with the artist—but most are on large sheets of opaque commercial vellum in a velvet-black charcoal moved very fast across the sheet. It leaves a rich, heavy mark which can be lightened to a whisper or pushed down to a mineral black. And it also has something of the nervous quality of his brush marks, thus becoming a practical approach to problems in the paintings.

Some of the drawings (twenty-four have been published as a separate book) are a strange, automatic series unique in de Kooning's oeuvre. Done on 8½-by-11-inch sheets of paper, they are attempts to start from scratch—to work on the Cartesian tabula rasa. All are of figures. Some were done with the artist's left hand, sometimes he did not look at the paper, sometimes he kept his eyes shut. The image comes out very fast, without control—or, better, without supervision, because the artist's mind and hand are full of experience, which implies control.

The practice is not a new one, of course; Leonardo da Vinci suggested it; many artists have practiced similar exercises, usually as a way of limbering up, or letting the hand surprise the eye.

De Kooning, however, has pushed the exercise much further. Often he starts a formal drawing by shutting his eyes and spinning the pencil around above the paper in a tight circle, then pressing down into a dot, out of which comes the shape. It is like setting off a little explosion. In these automatic drawings, however, he got the charcoal to flow across the paper smoothly, as if it was hooking a thought out of his brain.

He says, "If it didn't sound pompous, I'd call them Zen."

Zen archers, it will be remembered, do not aim at the target, but think about it, the bow and arrow held above their heads; then they bring their arms down and apart and when the bowstring is taut, let go.

These drawings are also a letting-go. And in the release, the images become some-how drenched with light. Indeed, it can be said that these are not studies of form, or of the figure, but of light—not only in the sense of an equivalence to (or paradigm of) luminosity set down as blacks on white, but also in de Kooning's very special definition of the quality, which will be discussed later in this essay.

Many of the little "Zen" drawings were done, eyes closed, while watching television. At other times de Kooning looked at the set. He especially enjoys the young dancers, Go-Go girls, and their gestures are caught in a number of drawings: knees spread, arms pumping, pelvis tilted, all rocking with that wide happy American smile.

There are also some drawings of TV singers, hitting the hard note, their hands pushing the sound as it comes out of their mouths.

Other subjects in the drawings include:

Some men with their arms spread out, as if in a crucifixion, with big noses and scowling faces (these pick up a theme de Kooning first worked with in the middle 1930s).

A striding male figure, with an important walk, which sometimes turns goofy as the man drops his arms to the side. In a few of these, de Kooning's lifelong love of, and admiration for, the funny papers is evident. He always has been fascinated by the idea of making a drawing into a character, like Dick Tracy, or better yet, some of the monsters in that strip, and then putting it through all the paces of a character in a melodrama. The drawing achieves a kind of prosaic grotesque which is at once comical, banal, and, in its way, great. "Of course the trouble with the Pop artists," de Kooning once said, "is that they don't pick the good funny papers."

A series on a reclining woman; she has one of those supersweet, heart-shaped Betty Boop (or Betty Grable) faces. She lies on the blank paper, or on a bed, or in the countryside, like a juvenile-delinquent odalisque. In some recent drawings she is sunbathing on a complicated modern beach lounge.

A seated woman, on the grass; knees together, feet apart, chin on her knees. Here the figure is reduced to the totem-pole alignment, but kept to a completely natural gesture. There are also indications of how summer clothes—shorts, shirts—fit on the body.

Complicated drawings with several figures in the landscape—talking together under the trees, sitting on the beach, having picnics, digging for clams, avoiding sunburns.

At first glance, of course, most of the drawings look abstract, and to those unfamiliar with de Kooning's style, they might have to be translated into such genre terms as those cited above. Furthermore, the inexperienced spectators who see mainly the patterns of light and varying speeds of line and who miss the subject matter may be seeing these works of art correctly. Phrasing them bit by piece into words does them a disservice—

the bad turn which criticism always plays on art. But it is important to emphasize that these works are circumstantial, and in their notations of a leg or a hat or a long April shadow, the artist is also seeking the elements of a new environment which will be the context of his art.

But they also stand on their own as independent work. The black charcoal is deployed across the page in masses and taut, swift lines; there is a flickering, dappled quality reminiscent of Venetian Renaissance drawings, particularly Titian's warm-bodied inflections.

Little Women

De Kooning's creative process cannot really be called a "process" (which implies a mechanical system), or even a working method; part of his idea is to keep everything up in the air at the same time, to make himself open, to let any idea that happens to be floating around have its chance. Thus to consider the drawings apart from the sketches and the small and large oils is to give a distorted impression of his approach—to rob it of its organic wholeness. But it would be impossible to describe the pictures in an accurate way without resorting to some kind of verbal assemblage or simultaneity of paragraphs, which would probably be as confusing as it might be correct. The smaller oils on paper, thus, can be considered as a group—as a step toward the large paintings—only with this caveat in mind: They are not really apart from any of the other pictures in either chronology or development. They are simply another aspect of an oeuvre which is extraordinary in its unity and cohesion.

The small oils are as finished as the drawings. They are, however, more formal, in the sense that de Kooning draws anywhere, anytime, but he paints in his studio. And despite their completeness and independence as objects, they do lead, in a way, toward the major statements.

In the drawings, shapes often relate directly to subject matter. The content may be "light" (in both meanings of the word), but the motif is something seen or re-created by the memory. In the oils, the drawings themselves are usually the things seen, or they are based on a combination of drawings (he also studies them one on top of the other, the sheets being just transparent enough to let a drawing underneath come through), or on interrelationships between drawings and the memory of a glimpse at nature that arrested him.

They often are painted on sheets of paper 18 by 23 inches; sometimes they are as large as 50 by 42; sometimes de Kooning will start with an image on one sheet, and it will expand as he paints it, so he adds another sheet below—resulting in a group of figures whose torsos are placed bang on top of a pair of legs.

He uses his regular repertory of oil colors and his favorite brushes whose long hairs bend into an S as the pigment is applied.

De Kooning's palette is organized in about eighty porcelain jars of colors he has pre-mixed himself, each with its special recipe, using regular commercial oil paints as ingredients. He started working out this system from a dissatisfaction with the available tube earth-pigments, which dry unevenly and leave a different finish from the mineral paints. With a few hints from the late Landes Lewitin, he decided to make earth colors out of mixtures of mineral ones, and, once he had established several basic hues, began to "breed" them with each other, ending up with an enormous family of hues. Some are strange off-colors ("This one is just like boiled liver," he said of an innocent-looking brownish-gray); others are keyed up to the maximum intensity for oil paints. He has never used plastic paints, and probably never will; his problem is that even oils dry too fast for him to keep working the destructions on his pictures which are so much a part of his approach. Plastic colors dry in a half hour and their body does not offer the resistance he needs. Essentially they offer technical shortcuts. De Kooning always insists on taking the long way around. His medium is an emulsion of safflower oil, benzine, and water. When properly mixed, the fluid is thick and foamy; when the water dries out, it is apt to leave areas of tiny bubble holes in the dried paint—it looks a bit like fine volcanic rock. De Kooning does not mind this side effect, and he likes the way his medium stays fresh for weeks at a time and dries evenly to a semimat surface with the texture of something like the skin of a healthy child: very few highlights, no dead spots.

There are almost no drips in the small pictures; de Kooning's brushstroke can control the complete laying down of the pigment. In the larger pictures, where the artist's arm gestures are broader and the amount of paint laid down heavier, drips will fly off the brush and streak down the picture. De Kooning says that he doesn't want them particularly, but he also doesn't want to tidy up after himself; so he leaves them there. It is possible that they add a sense of energy or anguish to the image; this is another side effect, like the pitted impastos his medium causes. They obviously add to the vulnerable, spontaneous look of the painting, which de Kooning probably enjoys. The point is that he tries to make his own accidents as he works and to make them fit his own experience; any other accidents are simply there, like a part of nature, or like the accidents which control how a painting will happen to look twenty years after it is finished.

The small oils have a much more restricted range of subject matter than the drawings: parts of the body (feet, legs, torsos), seated women, standing women, pairs of women, women in a landscape, a few landscape abstractions.

The Women have the goofy hilarity of the drawings, especially when seen as a group. It is as if de Kooning has invented a race of people; they have their own proportions, anatomies, and also their own joys and sorrows. They are very human, but they are all de Kooning. Because they are so many, and have such a strong family resemblance, in a group they are very funny. One is reminded of Flaubert's famous letter in which he talks about the artist walking a tightrope between the twin abysses of the lyric and the comic. When they are seen by themselves, the comic effect is much fainter. The fusion of the woman in color is the most evident drama you see; then the formal quality resulting from the fusion; finally one grasps the underlying gesture.

Every shape, de Kooning has said, even the most abstract one, must have a "likeness." One asks, Likeness to what? The only answer would be to invoke an interior logic. Perhaps the difficulty can be clarified by a reverse example. Take the famous mobiles of Alexander Calder—witty, beautiful, ingenious, lyrical—one could add a whole list of glittering adjectives. But one issue would remain—Calder has never invented a single form. This petal shape is from Miró; that squiggle is out of Léger; Mondrian colors here; Picasso there. It is one way (and there is nothing wrong with it) of approaching art. De Kooning, on the other hand, has to invent each shape—hand, eye, shoulder, even fingernails. And he has to do it with a hyperawareness of all other art—otherwise the invention would be primitive; beautiful but provincial. (De Kooning has a favorite anecdote about a man who spent his life working on a very complicated mechanism, and when he finally finished, it turned out that he had invented the harpsichord. He tells the story with a certain amount of admiration for the man, but he himself is an old pro at patent-searches.)

A small format, obviously, is much easier to control. It is possible to work within this scale and achieve a relatively huge motion of color in a ten-inch stroke. De Kooning is less obsessed with corrections in his small oils; the mistakes have their own value and he leaves them be. He can adjust a form by a line, without having to rip the whole color apart. He keeps them going, destroys the ones he gets tired of and doesn't like, and lets them move him while he brings them to completion. Thus the first environmental elements for Woman emerged in these works; they are marshes, trees, or hills, with roads and the ocean, sun and sky. But the shapes are new for de Kooning, close to the anatomies of Woman, and are given colors which are so exactly located that they must symbolize for the artist a given place or a precise vision. In one study, the figure has come into the landscape and reclines in it with the poise and raised arms of a Rubens river goddess.

Women and The Visit

The small oils on paper are often titled "Study" or "Sketch," even though they are usually created completely independently of any single larger work. What does distinguish them from the major oils of Women is that they are done without corrections, as it were in a single breath. The Women, on the other hand (and some of them are smaller than some of the Studies) involve all of the artist's arsenal of means and especially his needs to efface and repaint, destroy and re-create, over a long period of time, until the sum of erasures add their own density to the image. For the spectator, it is not a matter of sympathizing with the quarts of sweat that have gone into a technique; de

Kooning keeps his surfaces as fresh as a Lautrec. Nor is there a labored quality (as there is in certain Mondrians, for example, where you sense the intellectual struggle that went into fixing a yellow rectangle on exactly the right spot). Rather the painting gives a feeling of images lost, calling like ghosts behind the one presented on the canvas, and, most of all, of a certain historical gravity, very much a part of de Kooning's ambitions to work in the highest modes of art.

Something of his procedure can be reconstituted in a series of about twenty remarkable color photographs taken by de Kooning's assistant of *The Visit* during its development on the artist's painting-wall in the winter of 1966–67. The moments of development he recorded are not formal stages in the painting's evolution (as Matisse, for example, had photographs made of several of his works in progress at times that he felt were important to a demonstration of his ideas). The assistant would simply come into the studio to help out in the mornings, and if the picture looked interesting he would shoot it. It is an outsider's interpretation of the process, which has its own objective value.

There are almost no constant elements in the 5-by-4-foot picture during the months of its development. The hip shapes in the lower center, although changed in color and shape, remain as a dim point of focus almost throughout. The legs branch out at 90 degrees, then angle down parallel to the canvas edge in a rather froglike squat, which has its origin, of course, in *M. Bertin* by Ingres, one of de Kooning's great heroes. The figure is seated on a rocklike, or mound, form, which at first had a strange development into a half-face with a tilted mouth, then became the boxlike pedestal of a chair, and finally disappeared into paint whose directional strokes indicate that something solid is holding this very solid figure in position.

As for the face, it appears to change in the photographs like a stop-action sequence

I

II

Five stages from the photographic record of *The Visit* in progress. 1966–67

of Spencer Tracy turning into Mr. Hyde—only the Woman does not become hideous, just different. The head faces front, then to the left, then front again, then to the right; finally front with a tilt to the right. The hair goes from brunette to blond to red. Finally a hat is added. The mouth starts as a thin streak, slowly gapes open to reveal teeth, becomes closed and heavy in a pout, ends in an archaic smile. The shape of the head itself starts as an oval pushed in from the top and bottom; spreads out; then is elongated with the paint cutting deeply into the cheeks, and finally assumes a harlequin-diamond shape. Several times during this development, heavy masks of dark brown cover the features.

But the most dramatic changes are in the arms. They start out raised and spread outward from the elbows behind the Woman's head. At one point the arm on the left side of the picture appears down across the torso, ending in a large red hand. The right arm extends to the right edge in a hand with pointing fingers. It finally is moved down, to give more room to the right side of the painting, where the critical problem is being worked out.

At first, at the right, the artist sketched in a blocky tree-shape. This was soon wiped out and replaced, first by the Woman's hand, then by very active abstract-landscape forms, which slowly evolved into the face of a second figure. After this decision, the face stayed in the upper right-hand corner, until it was effaced again by a mass of flesh-color. Then the face came back in a rough drawing, with lowered eyelids, pointed nose, and rouged lips, all on green. The final resolution is a shape which could be the raised hand of the central figure or a face (there are indications of an eye in the opening of the fist).

Thus *The Visit* may refer to the appearance of the second figure in the painting and its ultimate destruction, or to the possibility that the second figure is still there, visiting the Woman, but partially hidden by her hand. Or, the Woman, with her arms

III   IV   V

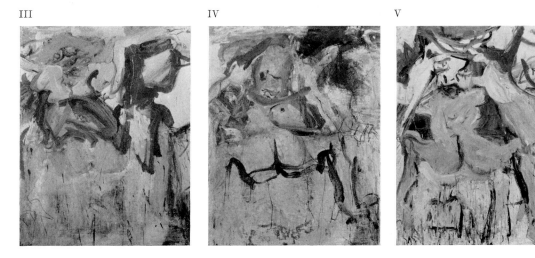

akimbo in a welcoming gesture, may be greeting a visitor who is entering her field of vision from just over the right shoulder of the spectator.

For what it is worth, the photographs record the appearance of the Visitor and that she was shy, humble, hesitant in front of the Woman, whose own expressions of, as they changed, serenity, erotic invitation, rage, sorrow, and a quizzical triumph always made her the dominant partner.

The landscape elements are kept abstract, indicating only a place in the countryside, but between the two figures a strong shape is developed, which is a tree or a rock but which echoes the Woman's shapes and partakes of her compelling organic strength.

A comparison of the colors and units of shape between *The Visit* and the other Women in 1964–67 with *Pastorale* and the abstract landscapes which preceded it indicates that de Kooning has gone back to smaller, more complicated shapes and inter-lockings, which recall his black and white abstractions of 1947–50, and to brighter, deeper colors. The concept of simplicity as a means has been abandoned. Unity of effect, however, has been reinforced by the change. The figure, with its central focus, comes across in a crescendo, like one huge dissonant chord played by a whole orchestra.

In the other major paintings of Women a similar gravity and complexity is implied. The image is brought into equilibrium with the paint, and as the paint gets more ferocious, the Woman does, too.

"I guess I am an Expressionist," de Kooning said, ruefully, looking at one of his more fantastically distorted figures. It is a position and a style for which he has no sympathy at all; he detests the corny Weltschmerz, egocentric pathos of Expressionism, especially its German varieties. And he avoids its sentimentality by insisting on the high comic side of the equation. In this he is very close to another happily *émigré* artist, James Joyce, who also made the distance necessary for a masterpiece by keeping laughter in his art.

If de Kooning is an Expressionist, he is unlike all the others in that loose category because he brings up his image from inside. Nolde or Soutine or Jorn or Bacon, to give examples from Germany, France, Denmark, and England, look outside, at life. The violence of their Expressionism is usually one of tear-stained regret or wet-eyed horror at the situation they confront in the world. De Kooning looks in, seeking what he is stuck with, his own light.

The Women crowd around the wall of de Kooning's still-unfinished studio in The Springs. It is a huge room built around steel struts designed like a seagull's wingspread. The walls are painted white. Light comes streaming in from glass on both sides of the painting-wall. The studio is lined with benches whose seats raise to allow storage space beneath for pounds of colors and brushes. Tables made from steel girders (painted steel-girder orange) are mounted on casters like an operating table's; their glass tops are his palette. Drawings are stored on the shelves beneath. The white terrazzo floor is protected by a roll of plastic which is fixed behind the painting-wall and unwinds across the room

The Visit. 1967. Oil on canvas, 60 × 48 in.

to a table and a rocking chair where there are cigarettes and coffee. It marks the path which de Kooning paces up and down, to and from his painting.

Behind the studio is a kitchen and to the south a living room with a massive fireplace which the artist keeps redesigning.

He has designed everything in his studio, and he works on it as he does on a painting: tearing walls down, moving cabinets around. A number of young artists have been hired to be his helpers. They were nicknamed "de Kooning's Peace Corps." One visitor rummaging around came across a drawer lined with small, neat compartments. "What's it for?" De Kooning said, "Why, collar studs." When asked if he owned so many studs, he admitted that a particular carpenter he employed was really only good at, and enjoyed, making little wood compartments.

Of course, de Kooning has been teased about his studio. But it is one of the most remarkable buildings of the twentieth century, moving, as it does, his loft space into the country. Like his art, it is impersonal, but completely original and every inch his own.

Only immigrants understand America, and only an artist who had moved for some forty years from rented studio to rented studio could have made this so new an edifice. It probably never will be finished to his satisfaction.

Nature

There are things an artist is stuck with, and there are choices open to him. De Kooning, for example, is stuck with the fact that he is a marvelous draftsman, just as Jackson Pollock was stuck with the fact that he had tremendous difficulty with drawing. It is not a matter of innate facility—Cézanne had no facility, but made great drawings; Boldini was a tiger of natural talent, but his drawings are weak and caricatural. Perhaps it is the brain in the wrist—a highly developed, self-critical center of physical actions, which works faster than the brain in the head can predict—that takes over? At any event, de Kooning visualizes through drawing; it is his means of perception; as much a part of himself by now as his train of associations or the timbre of his voice.

He is also stuck with what he calls his "light."

Light is a singular concept in postwar New York art. It means a number of things, some of them very vague and private. The word has replaced *space* in artists' talk; they refer to a "landscape light" instead of space, or Vermeer's light. *Space*, evidently, has too much of the formalist's materialism about it; it is a dimension that can be measured; an element in picture-making; a part of the techniques.

Light, on the other hand, is at once a more precise description or metaphor and a more slippery term.

First of all, and most obviously, it relates to location, to the place where the painting is made. Philip Pavia often talks about the importance of "Atlantic light" to New York art. De Kooning once was asked why he didn't take it easy in Florida in the winters and he replied that you would never catch him away from his northern light.

When you hear that there is "Paris light" in a Renoir or a Giacometti, it makes a certain sense. You infer a set of generally accepted hypotheses. But Renoir's light is 1880; Giacometti's is 1950. Here again, there are certain easy explanations. Mid-twentieth-century light has the experience of the bright electric glare. Nineteenth-century light remembers the gas lamp. Seventeenth-century light is a candle. And beyond a sense of place and time, light indicates a commonly held style. The Cubists' light, for example, is very different from that of their Parisian contemporaries, the Fauves.

Finally, there is the individual's unique quality; what de Kooning calls "my light" when he explains what he is trying to capture in a painting or drawing.

Light is the artist's own inflection of the common language of his own historical moment and his own geography. It is the content of his painting.

"Content," he has said, "is very small; it is a glimpse." At another time he called himself a "slipping glimpser."

"I was looking at something," he wrote recently. "I am by myself . . . nobody else is in it. I am just standing or sitting and looking. . . . At the most obvious . . . the sun going down for instance . . . as with almost anyone else . . . it can make you melancholy.

"One of the strongest sensations I had, and always comes back to me, was to look at some 'leftover' piece of ground.

"It had to do with the suburbs . . . the whole thing is very ordinary!

"Looking out of a little window at some leftover piece of ground . . . at nothing . . . maybe at a few empty Coke bottles or a beer can . . . the melancholy part has become delightful. . . ."

It's an old-fashioned way of putting it, perhaps, and he may be an old-fashioned artist. But perhaps fashion has lost its watch. Because if de Kooning is stuck with some things, where he has the freedom to make a choice he has invariably opted for the radical, vanguard position.

He joins with modern painters in that curious ethos of the picture plane. It is an esthetic judgment so final that its force can only be described as moral. For de Kooning, the paint *must* be on the surface; he rejects any form of illusionism. Each color or shape, as we have seen, has to be "made abstract again" before it can appear in the painting.

But if it is abstract, why the subject matter of a Woman, and the landscape elements; the anatomies and environments?

It is impossible today to paint a face, pontificated the critic Clement Greenberg around 1950.

"That's right," said de Kooning, "and it's impossible not to."

A deeper vanguard idea which de Kooning chooses is that of openness and liberty. He insists that anything is possible, that history is open, that all ideas are permissible—except those of exclusivity.

Of course, he is not quite as tolerant as he would seem. Not only must his own painting respect the picture plane and submit to a discipline of abstraction; de Kooning also rejects *retardataire* ideas—neo-Realisms, neo-Symbolisms, and others—not as necessarily without qualities, but as irrelevant.

History, in other words, does have certain imperatives for the artist; it is important, however, that they are not framed as suffocating dogma.

Simplistic formulations ("purity is to will one thing") and doctrinaire language make him sick because they lie about the world as he knows it: immensely complicated, mysterious, unmanageable, always shifting aspects; like Proteus, as soon as you think you have your hands around a throat, it changes and eludes your grip.

Lately de Kooning has been reading a book about molecules, which he finds very cheering. Before World War II, he explains, most physicists felt that they could tell you the number of components in an atom—a neutron, a proton, an electron, and so on. Today, he notes happily, no reputable physicist would even guess at the number. Furthermore, he is delighted to learn that molecules slip around a lot. A molecule of white paint on his studio wall, for an instance, could be a molecule of bread, with the loss of a particle so vague that it is practically metaphysical.

Nothing is sure, except that you have your own nature which forces you to paint in certain ways, and that you choose sides ("I don't know where it's going," he once said, "but I'm on the same train as Marcel Duchamp"—not that he has too much respect for Duchamp's art; it's just that one of Duchamp's paintings was reproduced in an issue of *Life* that was being discussed at the time). For the rest, in Barnett Newman's phrase, you are "alone in the studio."

The "Novel Gothic"

De Kooning chose the avant-garde, and gave it a new lease on life, because it represents the position of the free individual.

The idea goes back to the Renaissance and to the first emergence of what Dante called "the new painting."

The big fight of the Renaissance artist was not only to develop his own art and theory, but to break free from the medieval concept of the artist.

The painter and sculptor in feudal society worked happily as one of many specialists in a closed, homogeneous society. His work was often anonymous—he cut one more stone for the building of the Chartres cathedral, he added faces to a crowded composition, he applied gold leaf, he carved a demon at the bottom of a Last Judgment. He accepted his role in society with the same ease with which he accepted the whole bureaucracy of Gothic life: the pyramidal structures of the Church, the class structure, his own guild and its disciplines and rituals. His life was hierarchical; his goal was the work worthy of its hire and its ultimate payment—Heaven.

The Renaissance artist struggled to break loose from feudal constrictions. He would be an artist on his own; his discipline would not relate to artisanship, but be worthy of a place among the liberal arts. His social role would be the equal of the intellectual's—the doctor's, the judge's, the general's.

At first his responsibility was to Art; by the eighteenth century, his responsibility was to himself—in the existentialistic situation where a man must develop to the fullest whatever is within him, and anything that distracts him from this search for identity must be sacrificed—even if it means abandoning his family (Gauguin), his country (Goya), his sanity (van Gogh), his life (Pollock).

But all through these centuries of development, the artists had a strong nostalgia for the Gothic, one of the greatest ages in the history of art, and for the lost paradise of feudal existence.

The costume of the modern artist—perhaps it would be better to call it his uniform —is a workingman's clothes (as a matter of fact, recently it was the shoes, pants, shirt, jacket, and hat of the Paris workingman, beret, sandals and all; now it is changing and New York artists are apt to dress like skyscraper construction workers). Artists are drawn to workingmen's bars; they like their slang. The idea of craftsmanship still haunts most painters (even when they can't hammer a nail without putting it through their finger, they talk a good carpentry). And most of all, in moments of weakness and sentimentality, they long to be back in society with a given role, an assigned identity, roots.

Gothic revivals have marked modern art since its inception. There are the well-known cases of the Pre-Raphaelite Brotherhood and the concepts of Morris and Ruskin which grew out of it, and the German Nazarenes' medieval establishment in Rome, to say nothing of Gothic Revival architecture and design, especially where it poignantly decorates the most advanced bits of technology (i.e. the Gothic sprockets in steel which punctuate the Fifty-ninth Street Bridge in Manhattan). The case of the Bauhaus has not, as far as I know, been considered in this light, probably because of the brilliance with which its protagonists advertised it as the great school of modernity. But Gothic ideas permeated the Bauhaus—the concept of anonymity, the unsigned work, the artist collaborating with factory hands to produce a new craftsmanship, the idea of the artists' community (a technological guild), to say nothing of the medieval flavor which characterizes so much of its art and thought: Lyonel Feininger's paintings of Gothic ruins seen through Cubist grids; Mies van der Rohe's lectures on the integrity of the simple mason and his honest brick, the Gothicism inherent in the visions of Paul Klee.

Today we are perhaps at the watershed of history. It may not be the second Renaissance, which has been proclaimed so eagerly by a number of young backers of the New. Rather we may be witnessing the collapse of the Renaissance and the final triumph of the feudal. Artists are no longer merely nostalgic for the Gothic; they have decided to give up all the storms and stresses inherent in the Renaissance position, and go back to the Gothic.

After all, the Renaissance idea is very uncomfortable. One is alienated, alone except for a few friends, who are apt to be nutty. Every day brings new struggles and anguished doubts. One has to fight everything—art, society, one's self.

For the new feudalists, these uncertainties are henceforth resolved. First of all, the artist makes his peace with society. He is no longer a rebel; he swings with the rest of the scene. He is not embattled, except to get a good job, a comfortable house for his wife and children, and a raise every two years.

The lacerating concept of identity is let go; the new artist likes to work anonymously. He may keep his name on the work (he almost has to if he wants to sell it), but he will try to keep himself out of it. Sometimes this will mean he orders the piece from a factory to his specifications. Sometimes he will join a team of artists to make group products.

Where society can produce a patron (skyscraper-lobby architects, airport designers, government sponsors), the "Novel Gothic" artist is eager to meet all his specifications.

And the art world is a microcosm of the big cultural, economic, political world—and here we also see that life is reverting to the Gothic.

The hippies with their daffodils and bliss—what are they but the Children's Crusade, dreaming of Bosch's *Garden of Earthly Delights*.

And the verticality of our cities? I don't mean New York (it may have grown up the way it did because of the narrowness of Manhattan Island) so much as smaller cities like Houston, which rise out of a plain in a cluster of towers around which little buildings are crowded. It is the silhouette of Chartres. America is becoming full of towns that look like San Gimignano or Amiens.

Bureaucracies are taking over our lives: enormous hierarchies with ranks and rituals. Everything is assigned a place and a role.

The universal man gives way again to the specialist who works as a part of the team.

Thinking, too, becomes medieval—Thomist-Aristotelian rather than Neoplatonic; we go by what we know to be true rather than what we know for ourselves. Knowledge is so specialized that authorities are accepted without demur. The citizen cannot question a President on foreign policy because "only he has all the information" which it would be dangerous to release to the public: a formulation which has its percedent in the medieval concepts that forbid the layman to read the Bible or even to understand the mass; an expert is needed to deal with life-and-death questions.

Popular intellectual theories today, like those of McLuhan, have a utopian, encyclopedic ambition and attraction: a college freshman's summa. In the art world, young writers are attracted to deterministic formalist interpretations, which are medieval in their catechisms and ready answers. They trace history as easily as the old geographers drew charts of the known world.

Are we at the end of five hundred years of individualism? Will the next century be vinyl Gothic?

Marx and Santayana agree that when history repeats itself, it does so in terms of farce. But neither of them foresaw the communications mediums of today and the electronic speed with which history is whipped along. Things move so fast, events supersede one another so rapidly that history moves without friction or dialectical tensions. It becomes chronology—not a sequence of ideas and challenges, but a chronicle of what has happened lately.

And if this is so, is it so bad?

Perhaps the Renaissance idea was wasteful; men burn themselves out in an absurd fight for the unattainable. And, as Lord Keynes said, in the long run we are all dead. Perhaps people are happier doing what they are told and having everything they do labeled, organized, and planned.

And if this is so, it leaves de Kooning in the vanguard with his friends and colleagues (Barnett Newman, Mark Rothko, Adolph Gottlieb, Philip Pavia, Reuben Nakian, et al, and the younger painters and sculptors around them) as the last of the Renaissance: the old-fashioned moderns.

So it is most appropriate that de Kooning's pictures of the 1960s are drained of the anguish and look of despair which had so profoundly marked his earlier work. In the new Women, the mood is Joy.

I like the idea: to end an epoch with a burst of laughter.

And if the new feudalism is merely one more episode in a chaotic century, to be superseded itself, and if the Renaissance concept will prevail, what better link for continuities could there be than de Kooning's sun-flecked girls and goddesses?

Two Women. 1964. Oil on paper, 60 × 35 in. The Joseph H. Hirshhorn
Collection

Wading Woman. 1965. Oil on paper, 28½×22½ in. Collection John G. Powers

Woman Sag Harbor Small. 1965. Oil on paper, 31×19 in. Collection John G. Powers

Woman Springs. 1966. Oil on wood, 80×36 in.
Collection Edgar Kaufmann, jr.

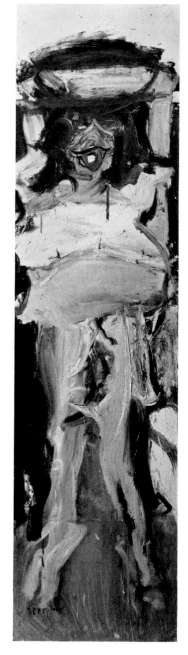

Singing Woman. 1965. Oil on paper, 88×24 in.
Collection John G. Powers

Woman in Landscape. 1966. Oil on paper, 32×20 in.   *Singing Women*. 1966. Oil on paper, 36×24 in.

Figure in Marsh Landscape. 1966. Oil on canvas, 25 × 30 in.

Women Singing II.
1966. Oil on paper,
36×24 in.

Figure in Landscape. 1966.
Oil on paper, 22½×28½ in.

Figure in Landscape. 1966.
Oil on canvas, 30×25 in.

Figure in Watermill Landscape. 1966.
Oil on canvas, 25×30 in.

Clam Digger. 1966.
Oil on paper, 42×29 in.

Brancusi. 1966. Oil on newspaper, 37 × 26 in.

Pink Woman Torso. 1967. Oil on paper,
23 × 18¼ in.

Pink Standing Figure. 1967. Oil on paper,
23 × 18¼ in.

Standing Figure in Yellow. 1967. Oil on paper,
23 × 18¼ in.

Standing Figure in Brown. 1967. Oil on paper,
23 × 18¼ in.

Figure in Water. 1967. Oil on paper,
23 × 18¼ in.

Dubliner. 1967. Oil on paper, 39¼ × 18 in.

Woman in the Water. 1967. Oil on paper,
23 × 18¼ in.

Standing Figure in Marsh Landscape.
1967. Oil on paper, 23×18¼ in.

Snake Charmer. 1967. Oil on paper, 34×24 in.

Figure with Red Hair. 1967. Oil on paper,
23×18¼ in.

55

Man. 1967. Oil on paper, 56 × 41¾ in.

Color for Blonde Woman. 1966.
Oil on canvas, 30× 25 in.

Running Figure. 1966. Oil on paper,
24× 22½ in.

Study for Landscape. 1967. Oil on paper, 23×18¼ in.

Woman Montauk. 1967. Oil on paper, 31¾×26½ in.

Marsh Landscape. 1966. Oil on canvas, 30×25 in.

Reclining Figure in Marsh Landscape. 1967. Oil on paper, 18¼×23 in.

Two Figures Standing. 1967. Oil on paper, 31½×26¼ in.

Woman in the Garden II. 1967. Oil on paper, 23×18¼ in.

Woman in the Garden I. 1967. Oil on paper, 41¾×29½ in.

60

Woman on a Sign I. 1967. Oil on paper, 48½×36¼ in.

Woman on a Sign II. 1967. Oil on paper, 56×41¼ in.

Woman on a Sign III. 1967. Oil on paper, 41¾×37½ in.

Woman on a Sign IV. 1967. Oil on paper, 23¼×18½ in.

Woman and Child. 1967. Oil on paper, 52¾ × 47½ in.